3

Roadside
Wildflowers
of the Northwest

Flowering Dogwood

by J.E.(Ted)Underhill

ISBN 0-88839-108-0
Copyright © 1981 J.E. Underhill

Canadian Cataloging in Publication Data
  Underhill, J.E., 1919-
    Roadside wildflowers of the northwest

    ISBN 0-88839-108-0

    1. Wildflowers - British Columbia - Identifi-
    cation.   2. Roadside flora - British Columbia
    - Identification.   I. Title.
    QK203.B7U5   582.13'09711
    C81-091117-5

Fourth Printing 1989

Editor Margaret Campbell
Production Peter Burakoff
Layout/Design Diana Lytwyn
Typeset by Sandra Sawchuk and Anne Whatcott in Megaron type on
an AM Varityper Comp/Edit

Cover photo credits: upper left - B.C. Parks
                      middle left - B.C. Parks
                      middle right - Wm. Merilees
                      lower left - Al and Jude Grass
                      lower right - J.E. Underhill

Printed in Hong Kong

Published simultaneously in Canada and the United States by

HANCOCK HOUSE PUBLISHERS LTD.
19313 Zero Ave., Surrey, B.C. V3S 5J9
HANCOCK HOUSE PUBLISHERS
1431 Harrison Avenue, Blaine, WA 98230

Table of Contents

Introduction

Roadways, as we all know, are for exploration and discovery! It is only by means of roadways that most of us have been able to move out over this vast region to admire its mountains and rivers, to see its wild animals, and to discover its native and introduced wildflowers.

But as roadways have freed us, they have freed the animals and wildflowers too. Think about it. Roadsides are man-made strips of open land that often differ markedly from the forest or swamp through which they pass. They are thus artificial corridors on which animals and plants live and move where they could not have gained a foothold on the original terrain. Roadsides are indeed special places!

This book is for people who travel our area, and who want an easy and reasonably sure way to put names to the more conspicuous and common of the plants they meet along the roads of the northwest. It must be emphasized that only about 100 of the region's 2000 or so kinds of flowering plants are included here. Nevertheless, the showy and common flowers that most people notice will generally be found on these pages. Omitted are hundreds of rare or inconspicuous kinds, and species of very limited distribution or plants not likely to be seen close to major roads.

Books for more serious botanists list plants by plant families, often widely separating kinds with very similar appearance. Here, however, "look-alikes" are brought together to make identification easier and quicker for the untrained reader. The plants are presented in the order of the flower color. We start with the biggest group, the white flowers, then proceed through cream to yellow to orange to scarlet to red and pink to rose to mauve and purple to blue, and finally to a few odd species which have green or brown flowers, or are included because of spectacular foliage.

In addition, an attempt has been made to group plants that are apt to be found growing together.

English plant names have always been a problem. There has never been a list of them that has succeeded in gaining acceptance over any wide area. Instead, many plants have acquired local names in the many different areas in which the species grows. Thus our own *Erythronium oregonum* goes by the three names "Curly Lily," "Easter Lily," and "Dog-tooth Violet" in different parts of Vancouver Island alone. Elsewhere it has still other names. This results in some very vociferous arguments!

In an effort to produce at least local consistency, this book follows the English plant names advocated by the late Lewis J. Clark in his classic work *The Wild Flowers of British Columbia*. The Latin names are far more consistent. The ones used here accord with *Flora of the Pacific Northwest*, Hitchcock and Cronquist, with some minor simplifications.

We urge you to remember that the roadside wildflowers are not yours, like the ones in your garden, but ours, like the ones in our parks. Please don't pick them. Leave them alone —all of them — for the rest of us to enjoy with you!

Picking is by no means the only hazard roadside wildflowers must face. Even worse is the powerful spraying of roadsides with 2-4-D and other powerful weedicides. In some areas spraying has been carried out so regularly for the past twenty years that virtually all roadside wildflowers have been eliminated and only spray-tolerant grasses remain. To the discerning eye, spray damage is sometimes evident many feet back from the road amongst the forest plants.

But such is the vitality of most plants that many hundreds of miles of roadsides, especially in more rural areas, still retain their flowers. If you watch these flowers year by year you will get to know them, and you may observe how they, like you, travel the roads. Along the roads there is always something new to find.

FLOWERING DOGWOOD
Cornus nuttallii

- a tree of coastal slopes, where it flowers in late spring

This, B.C.'s provincial floral emblem, is a small forest tree. As in Dwarf Dogwood, the white parts are modified leaves.

EASTER LILY
Erythronium oregonum

- forest edge and light woodlands near the coast in spring

This popular plant has almost as many English names as there are places where it grows! Curly Lily, Dog-tooth Violet, Fawn Lily and Trout Lily are but a few. (See also Avalanche Lily and Pink Easter Lily pages 16 & 33.)

TRILLIUM
Trillium ovatum

- rich, moist woodlands at lower elevations in the spring

Trillium is protected by law in B.C., because picking it involves taking the leaves with the flower, so usually destroys the plant.

DWARF DOGWOOD
Cornus canadensis

- from sea level to timberline on forest edge, flowering in early summer

The white "petals" are actually leaves surrounding the tiny central cluster of insignificant flowers. In autumn there are scarlet berries and copper and bronze foliage.

QUEEN CUP
Clintonia uniflora

- forests at moderate elevations in the mountains in summer

The single (sometimes twin) flowers of this lily are followed by handsome berries that look like bright blue beads.

Credit: B.C. Parks

WILD STRAWBERRY
Fragaria spp.

- widespread on dry, open sites to considerable altitudes

This low-growing plant grows "runners" to create colonies. The white flower is handsome, and the ripe fruit, though small and seldom plentiful, is superb in flavor.

TALL WHITE REIN ORCHID
Habenaria dilatata

- swampy ground and ditches in early summer

The magnificent scent of this wild orchid is something special to experience. Probably it is the most highly perfumed of all our wildflowers. Stop and have a sniff!

Credit: B.C. Parks

MINERS' LETTUCE
Montia perfoliata (A)
Montia sibirica (B)

- moist forest edge to rock bluffs, flowering in spring

In *M. perfoliata* the upper leaves are joined to create a shallow bowl beneath the flowers. *M. sibirica* often has petals prettily striped with red. Both are very variable.

A

Credit: Al and Jude Grass

B

Credit: B.C. Parks

7

MOUSE-EARED CHICKWEED
Cerastium arvense

- dry situations from the coast to the Interior

Handsome mats of silvery-gray foliage with pure white flowers that have notched petal tips make this plant easy to know.

FRINGE CUP
Lithophragma parviflora

- widespread in dry grassy areas and coastal rock bluffs, with flowers in spring

The leaves are few, much divided, and inconspicuous, but the white or pinkish flowers are distinctive and attractive.

SNOWBRUSH
Ceanothus velutinus

- dry roadbanks, especially in the Interior, in early summer

The heavy, glossy, evergreen leaves are a handsome foil for the masses of tiny, whitish flowers. The leaves are often badly frost-burned in colder winters.

Credit: Wm. Merilees

Credit: Wm. Merilees

LABRADOR TEA
Ledum groenlandicum
L. glandulosum

- ditches and marshes throughout our area, blooming in early summer

Both species have similar white flowers. In both the leaves are glossy dark green above, but woolly beneath. In *L. groenlandicum* the "wool" is distinctly rusty-red, while in *L. glandulosum* it is almost white.

RED-OSIER DOGWOOD
Cornus stolonifera

- often abundant by creekbanks and lakeshores, flowering in early summer

The name refers to the bright red twigs, so evident in winter. The white flower "bouquets" of summer are succeeded by attractive clusters of blue-white berries. Autumn turns the leaves a handsome dark wine red.

Credit: Al and Jude Grass

SASKATOON BERRY
Amelanchier alnifolia

- throughout the northwest to considerable elevations

Saskatoon berry is usually seen as a shrub, but sometimes becomes tree-like in the B.C. Interior. Its dark purple berries were once much used by prairie Indians to make pemmican.

MOCK ORANGE
Philadelphus lewisii

- widespread, but most common along roadsides of the southern Interior, where it flowers in early summer

When in blossom this is an outstanding shrub. It is not surprising that nurserymen long ago selected and propagated the finest forms and made them available for our gardens. It should not be taken from the wild. Notice that some plants are delightfully sweet scented.

THIMBLEBERRY
Rubus parviflorus

- often abundant along forest edge, blossoming in early summer

Snow-white flowers like single roses give way to domed edible berries that ripen to a bright red.

OX-EYE DAISY
Chrysanthemum leucanthemum

- often carpets roadsides and meadows, flowering in early summer

This small, white, introduced Chrysanthemum is said to be part of the parental stock of the Shasta Daisy, so prized in our gardens.

Credit: Mrs. J.M. Woollett

Credit: Mrs. J.M. Woollett

Credit: B.C. Parks

PEARLY EVERLASTING
Anaphalis margaritacea

- widespread on open roadsides from the coast into the mountains, flowering in summer

The heads of flowers, first white then becoming chaffy, persist into autumn atop their unbranched, woolly stems. The narrow leaves, too, are very woolly.

Credit: B.C. Parks   Credit: Al and Jude Grass

MILFOIL
Achillea millefolium

- frequently encountered from the coast to the sub-alpine, has a long season of bloom

Pick one of the leaves, and see how finely divided it is. Smell its strong aromatic aroma. Like many strong-smelling herbs, it has a long history as a cure for various ailments.

Credit: Wm. Merilees   Credit: Al and Jude Grass

BIRCH-LEAVED SPIRAEA
Spiraea betulifolia

- common along forest edge, flowering in summer

This plant is quite distinctive, with its soft, flat, fuzzy flower clusters atop a woody stem that seldom exceeds 0.6 of a meter (two feet) in height.

FALSE SOLOMON'S SEAL
Smilacina racemosa

- damp forest edge in early summer

The handsome plume of creamy-white flowers is followed by a cloud of speckled berries that ripen red.

COW PARSNIP
Heracleum lanatum

- a common roadside plant, from moist forest edge to considerable elevations in the mountains

This is likely the largest of our roadside herbs, often growing taller than a man. Its nosegays of small white flowers are a prime attraction to a variety of insects in warm, sunny weather. The deadly Water Hemlocks look somewhat similar, but are smaller, and have finely cut leaves.

GOATSBEARD
Aruncus sylvester

- moist woodland edge west of the Cascades, flowering in early summer

Goatsbeard raises its striking creamy flowers as much as two meters (six feet) against the dark backdrop of the forest. The compound leaves, too, are attractive.

Credit: B.C. Parks

Credit: Al and Jude Grass

ALUMROOT
Heuchera. spp.

- rock crevices and roadsides, flowering in early summer

Spikes of creamy-white flowers above rosettes of toothed, heart-shaped leaves make this rock plant very attractive.

Credit: B.C. Parks

WESTERN MOUNTAIN ASH
Sorbus sitchensis

- widespread from the coast to near timberline, blooming in late spring

The compound leaves with seven to eleven leaflets, and the distinctly woody branches, help distinguish this shrub from the Elderberries (see below). The berries are pea-sized.

RED ELDER
Sambucus racemosa

- common along roads through woodlands west of the Cascades

This large shrub has pyramidal trusses of tiny flowers that are succeeded by little red berries. Hollow stalks and sharp-tipped leaflets distinguish it from Mountain Ash. Further east we have related kinds with blackish, yellow or white fruit.

Credit: Wm. Merilees

BLUE ELDER
Sambucus cerulea

- sporadic along the roadsides of southern B.C.

On this robust shrub the big flattish nosegays of tiny white flowers are followed by heavy clusters of little dark berries made conspicuous by a powdery blue dusting on their surface. The hollow stalks and leaflets with long sharp tips quickly differentiate this plant from Mountain Ash.

DEATH CAMAS
Zygadenus venenosus (A)
Zygadenus elegans (B)

- dry to moist open places in the spring — *Z. elegans* occurs in mountain country east of the Cascades, while *Z. venenosus* is more western (and has smaller and more yellowish flowers)

Death Camas has highly toxic bulbs that much resemble those of the edible Camas with which it often grows. Indians rightly respected it and tried to eradicate it from their Camas patches (see page 45).

A

Credit: Wm. Merilees

B

Credit: Al and Jude Grass

OCEAN SPRAY
Holodiscus discolor

- widespread to moderate elevations, especially in the S.W.

Massive sprays of creamy flowers soon turn brownish on this large shrub. The leaves are roughly triangular with rounded and toothed lobes.

Credit: B.C. Parks

YELLOW ARUM
YELLOW SKUNK
CABBAGE
Lysichitum americanum

- swampy places in early spring
The extremely large leaves have a strong smell when crushed. This smell attracts flies to pollinate the numerous tiny flowers of the club-like spadix.

AVALANCHE LILY
Erythronium grandiflorum

- high places in the Interior, blooming from spring into early summer as the snow line climbs
Avalanche Lily is often so eager that it sends its flowers up through the edge of the receding snow! (See also Pink Easter Lily and Easter Lily pages 33 & 5.)

Credit: B.C. Parks

VIOLET
Viola spp.

- grassy places and forest edge, with flowers in the spring
We have over a dozen kinds, with several yellow and one dark blue-purple predominating. White and pale violet species are less often seen by the roadside, but do occur. **(See also** *Viola adunca* **page 42.)**

Credit: B.C. Parks

Credit: Wm. Merilees

MONKEY FLOWER
Mimulus guttatus (A)
Mimulus alsinoides (B)

Common Monkey Flower *(M. guttatus)* is one of several yellow-flowered species in ditches and creeks from the coast to moderate elevations in the mountains.
Little Monkey Flower *(M. alsinoides)* blooms in spring on damp places on coastal rock bluffs.

A

B

YELLOW FLAG
Iris pseudacorus

- lake margins, streambanks and ditches in summer

This Iris escaped from gardens years ago, and is now widely established in our area.

Credit: Wm. Merilees

BLACK TWINBERRY
Lonicera involucrata

- frequent on moist open ground in mid elevations, blooming in late spring and early summer

On this shrubby Honeysuckle small yellow flowers are borne above twin "collars" termed bracts. These usually turn bright red in late summer, and eventually carry the twin shiny black berries.

Credit: B.C. Parks

COMMON MULLEIN
Verbascum thapsus

- locally common, particularly on roadsides of the dry Interior where it flowers in early summer

The big, woolly, basal leaf rosettes and tall spires of yellow flowers attract much attention. These plants were introduced from Europe, and enjoy dry gravelly ground.

BUTTER-AND-EGGS
Linaria vulgaris

- a widespread roadside immigrant
  from southern Europe
This looks like a slender, small yellow
Snapdragon with blue- green foliage. It
spreads both by seed, and by underground stolons that enable it to make
dense colonies.

Credit: Al and Jude Grass

PUCCOON
Lithospermum ruderale

- common in dry Interior valleys,
  where it blooms in early summer
We have two fairly similar species.
Both were once used by the Indians in
preparation of dyes.

Credit: Wm. Merilees

BLAZING STAR
Mentzelia laevicaulis

- hot, exposed places in Interior
  valleys, blooming early summer
Mentzelia is not too common, but is
included here because finding it is a
spectacular treat for the roadside
botanist. The fuzzy flowers may spread
to ten centimeters (four inches), but
they open only in the full sunshine of a
hot summer's day.

Credit: Al and Jude Grass

ST. JOHN'S WORT
Hypericum perforatum

- introduced from Europe and becoming widespread on open pastures and roadsides, flowers in summer

The species name calls attention to the dark dots on the petal edges and on the leaves. The plant is toxic, and has become a serious pest to stockmen.

Credit: Wm. Merilees

BROOM
Cytisus scoparius

- brought from Scotland to southern Vancouver Island in the mid 1800s, and now spreading on open land

Variations marked with deep red tones are fairly common.

Credit: Al and Jude Grass

YELLOW DRYAD
Dryas drummondii

- roadside gravels of the Rockies and the north in summer

Mats of Dryad's small, wrinkled, evergreen leaves are dark green above and white and hairy beneath. Golden flowers are succeeded by graceful plumed seed heads. We also have two kinds with whitish flowers.

BUTTERCUP
Ranunculus spp.

- meadows and ditchbanks in spring

Many species of the primitive buttercups brighten our roadsides. All have glossy golden petals that are *not* notched.

Credit: Wm. Merilees

STONECROP
Sedum spp.

- dry, exposed rock outcrops and rockslides, blooming in summer
Swollen, fleshy leaves are water-storage devices adapting Stonecrop to its spartan habitat. We have several kinds, most with starry yellow flowers.

OREGON GRAPE
Mahonia spp.

- well-drained woodland soils, blooming in early summer
Handsome sprays of small yellow flowers are followed by clusters of berries that have a bright blue powdery "bloom." The compound leaves somewhat resemble those of Holly.

Credit: B.C. Parks

SULPHUR FLOWER
Eriogonum umbellatum

- dry slopes of the Interior in early summer
We have several very variable Eriogonum species in the Pacific Northwest. The foliage is attractive, often silvery beneath, and red leaves are often evident.

ANTELOPE BUSH
Purshia tridentata

- dry Interior valleys, blooming briefly in spring
This large arid-land shrub has three-toothed green leaves, while those of the Sagebrush that grows with it are three-toothed but distinctly silver-gray.

Credit: B.C. Parks

RABBIT BRUSH
Chrysothamnus nauseosus

- dry Interior roadsides and slopes, blooming in autumn
Rabbit brush has deep yellow flowers and narrow, silvery leaves. It often grows with Sagebrush, which has greenish flowers, and leaves that are broadened with three points.

Credit: Wm. Merilees

Credit: Wm. Merilees

BALSAM ROOT
Balsamorhiza sagittata

- a feature of Interior valley slopes
when it flowers in spring
Balsam Root's big tufts of arrow-
headed leaves, with their silvery under-
sides, are always noticeable. When a
mass of them bedeck a hillside with
green and gold in spring they almost
compel a roadside stop!

ARNICA
Arnica spp.

- conspicuous along mountain
roadsides and in parts of the
Interior, flowering in early
summer
The several species are low to about
thirty-five centimeters (fourteen
inches) in height. All have deep golden
flowers, and opposite pairs of leaves of
a variety of shapes.

BROWN-EYED SUSAN
Gaillardia aristata

 - dry Interior valleys, blooming in summer

We have no other plant similar to this one. It has dark golden-yellow flowers with brownish centers, the ray petals doubly-cleft to give each three tips.

OYSTER PLANT
Tragopogon dubius

 - common along dry, sunny road-sides, flowering late spring and early summer

The yellow flowers are followed by big, puffy seed-heads that are conspicuous atop the slender blue-green foliage. The species was introduced here from Southern Europe.

Credit: B.C. Parks

Credit: Al and Jude Grass

GOLDENROD
Solidago canadensis

- general in our area, flowering in late summer

Goldenrod waves its yellow flag to signal that summer holidays are over and it is time to think of school once more!

PRICKLY PEAR CACTUS
Opuntia spp.

- a low-growing roadside plant in the Sagebrush country, in bloom late spring and early summer

Spiny cactus plants are a minor hazard for children and the family dog in parts of the dry Interior. One encounter with cactus teaches years of caution!

COLUMBIA TIGER LILY
Lilium columbianum

- forest glades and edges in early summer

Tiger Lily often grows in striking combination with dense colonies of blue lupine along our roadsides.

ORANGE HONEYSUCKLE
Lonicera ciliosa

- widespread along forest edge, where it blooms in late spring
Honeysuckle is most noticeable near the coast, where its vines often clamber five to six meters (fifteen to twenty feet) into the trees. Hummingbirds and butterflies are much attracted by the flamboyant flowers.

WESTERN COLUMBINE
Aquilegia formosa

- late spring and early summer on fairly moist, open ground
Like other red flowers, these are of great interest to hummingbirds, who sip nectar from the long spurs that extend behind the flowers.

INDIAN PAINTBRUSH
Castilleja spp.

- we have many kinds, occurring from coastal rock bluffs to high in the mountains, and blooming from late spring to mid summer
Paintbrush may be scarlet, rose, orange, yellow or white. All are partly parasitic upon adjacent plants. The bright-colored parts are modified leaves or "bracts" that surround the slender beak-like flowers.

Credit: B.C. Parks

SCARLET GILIA
Gilia aggregata

- common east of the Cascades on dry slopes and slides, with flowers in early summer

Despite its vivid flower color, this plant manages to be less than conspicuous because its small flowers are borne in an open spray. Sometimes it forms dense colonies that are then more readily seen.

Credit: Wm. Merilees   Credit: B.C. Parks

Credit: Mrs. J.M. Woollett

VETCH
Vicia spp.

- several kinds, mostly introduced here as fodder plants, and now established on open wasteland

These small relatives of the Peas have flowers of various colors. They are best distinguished from the Peas by the fact that their styles have little "bottle brush" tips.

PERENNIAL PEA
Lathyrus latifolius

- introduced from Europe and now widely established, especially near the coast; flowers in early summer

Perennial Pea offers masses of striking large flowers that vary from white to bright rose on different plants. These, with the winged stems and the tendriled, vigorous vines, make it easy to recognize.

SALMONBERRY
Rubus spectabilis

- common at the coast on damp
  ground, scarce inland, flowering
  in early to mid spring

Flowers of rose pink are succeeded by
edible fruit of raspberry form. The fruit
may be yellow or dark red.

WILD ROSE
Rosa spp.

- several species, widespread at
  lower levels, and flowering in
  early summer

Delicate pink blossoms are followed by
"hips" that ripen orange scarlet. These
make a jelly or jam of excellent flavor.

PINK
RHODODENDRON
Rhododendron macrophyllum

This handsome native shrub is seen as
a British Columbia roadside plant only
in the Skagit River basin, especially on
the western slopes of Manning Park,
and is the floral emblem of Washington
State. There it grows in mass, and puts
on a fine display in favorable years in
mid-June. It enjoys special legal
protection, and must not be picked or
dug up.

STICKY GERANIUM HAIRY GERANIUM

STICKY GERANIUM
Geranium viscosissimum

- dry roadsides of the Interior, flowering in early summer
As the name suggests, the whole sixty-centimeter (two-foot) tall plant is very sticky. There are several smaller-flowered and dwarf kinds that are quite common at the coast.

FIREWEED
Epilobium angustifolium

- throughout our area on burnt or disturbed ground, blooming in summer
Fireweed provides the beautiful, rosy healing blanket that conceals the wounded landscape, and shelters the seedlings of the herbs and shrubs that will join it in starting a new cycle of plants.

BEARBERRY
Arctostaphylos uva-ursi

- forest edge and open rocky places, flowering early summer
Flat, trailing evergreen mats of this shrub produce pink, urn-shaped blossoms that are followed by scarlet berries. At its best, this is one of our most ornamental native plants.

SALAL
Gaultheria shallon

- abundant along roads throughout coastal forests, with flowers from late spring well into summer

Salal's glossy, evergreen leaves, pink flowers, and purple-black edible berries made it a garden sensation when botanist David Douglas took it from here to England in the early 1800s.

Credit: B.C. Parks

SWAMP LAUREL
Kalmia microphylla

- widely distributed on boggy ground, with flowers in early summer

Showy deep pink flowers on bright red stems are borne above rather sparse foliage that somewhat resembles that of Labrador Tea. The two plants are related, and often grow together.

TWIN-FLOWER
Linnaea borealis

- to be seen along the edge of coniferous forest, where it blooms in early summer

Linnaea makes low mats of small shiny leaves that are an attractive foil for the pairs of delicate pink "trumpets." The name honors the great botanist Linnaeus, for whom this was a favorite plant.

Credit: Wm. Merilees

LARGE WINTERGREEN
Pyrola asarifolia

- common and widespread on coniferous forest edge, blooming in summer

This woodlander has basal rosettes of dark green, glossy leaves, rounded or roughly oval in shape. Above these the flower spikes rise to about forty centimeters (sixteen inches). Note the distinctive long curved style that protrudes from each flower.

PRINCE'S PINE
Chimaphila spp.

- roadsides through forests, flowering in early summer

Sparse clusters of small, clear pink flowers hang their heads above a few whorls of distinctive sharply-toothed, glossy, evergreen leaves.

BITTER ROOT (Spaetlum)
Lewisia rediviva

- from arid Interior valleys to high ridges in spring

The striking clusters of white to rich pink flowers huddle almost atop fleshy reddish roots that were once an important food for interior Indian people.

PINK EASTER LILY
Erythronium revolutum

- locally abundant on wooded flood-
  plains near the coast, flowering
  in spring

Bright, rose-pink, reflexed petals nod
atop a naked flower stalk. This, and the
handsome, marbled leaves, make the
plant easy to identify. (See also Easter
Lily and Avalanche Lily pages 5 & 16.)

SEA BLUSH
Plectritis congesta

- often abundant on coastal rock
  bluffs and meadows, where it
  flowers in spring

Massed drifts of Sea Blush, often
growing with Camas, or with Blue-
Eyed Mary, are a color treat for
springtime flower-watchers. Sea Blush
is an annual, and survives the summer
drought of the rock bluffs in its seed
stage — a handy arrangement!

Credit: Wm. Merilees

B

WILD ONION
Allium cernuum (A)
A. acuminatum (B) *& others*

- dry sites in mid-season

These attractive little lilies are true
onions, with all the smell of those from
the supermarket. Pinch a leaf and sniff
it!

FLOWERING RED CURRANT

WILD CURRANTS & GOOSEBERRIES
Ribes spp.

- seashore forest edge to moderate elevations in the mountains, blooming in late spring

Gooseberries have prickles, Currants do not. Both are members of the same large group of shrubs, many native to our area. All have leaves that are lobed and "maple-like." Showiest is Flowering **Red Currant** *(Ribes sanguineum)* of coastal slopes. Fruit of the various species is blue to red or greenish, and not enjoyable to eat.

STICKY CURRANT

STINK CURRANT

HARDHACK
Spiraea douglasii

- widespread in swampy places and ditches, with flowers in late spring

The soft columns of rich pink flowers soon turn dark brown.

HEDGE NETTLE
Stachys cooleyae

- moist places west of the Cascades, blooming in summer Colonies stand about 1.3 meters (four feet) tall, bearing leaves that rather resemble those of unrelated Stinging Nettles. Square stems and the flower form, however, mark *Stachys* as a mint rather than a nettle.

PINK MONKEYFLOWER
Mimulus lewisii

- flowers in summer in ditches and streams in the mountain passes The plant is named after Captain Meriwether Lewis of the Lewis and Clark expedition.

BLEEDING HEART
Dicentra formosa

- damp woodland edge, west of the Cascades, spring and early summer

Delicately cut blue-green leaves are an attractive foil for the odd but graceful flowers of this common woodlander.

SHOWY MILKWEED
Asclepias speciosa

- sporadic along roadsides of the dry Interior, flowering well into summer

This plant is remarkable for its abundant, sticky latex; for the way it compels insect visitors to carry off its pollen; and for its strange bond with the Monarch Butterfly, whose caterpillars feed solely upon Milkweed leaves.

SHOOTING STAR
Dodecatheon spp.

- several species, most flowering in spring on open, grassy places that have spring moisture but dry in summer

These are Primula relatives. Their flowers typically have five strongly reflexed petals, and they are carried on naked stalks above rosettes of basal leaves. Most of our kinds are purplish-pink, with one woodland species being white.

Credit: B.C. Parks

THISTLE
Cirsium spp.

Two thistle species are most noticeable. Canada Thistle spreads by underground roots to create dense colonies on roadsides and cultivated fields throughout our area. It is shoulder-tall, and has small, purple-pink flowers. Edible Thistle is more solitary, has more pronounced spines, and has large rose-purple flowers with many cobwebby hairs.

Credit: Al and Jude Grass

EDIBLE THISTLE

PINK PUSSY-TOES
Antennaria rosea

- common in wooded parts of the Interior, where it blooms in early summer

The flower color varies considerably, with some striking forms, as illustrated. In many other plants the color is rather dingy. We also have a variety of whitish *Antennarias.* The group, in general, has long, narrow, more-or-less woolly leaves.

Credit: Mrs. J.M. Woollett

ASTER
(Michaelmas Daisy)
Aster spp.

- widespread and conspicuous when it flowers in late summer

We have Asters in a considerable variety of species. Most have flowers of purple to mauve, varying to pink. For children the appearance of these flowers marks the end of summer holidays and the start of another school year.

KNAPWEED
Centaurea spp.

- an abundant roadside weed in dry Interior valleys, with flowers in summer

We have several fairly similar species of these introduced weeds. Most have small purplish to white flowers that remind us of the garden "Bachelor's Buttons." Foliage is stiff and bristly.

Credit: Al and Jude Grass

Credit: B.C. Parks

WILD BERGAMOT
Monarda fistulosa

- sporadic in the Interior valleys, blooming in early summer

This is our native relative of the Bee Balm of our gardens, which is a plant oi eastern North America. The leaves of Bergamot, dried and crushed, are an excellent herb with which to garnish a soup.

COLT'S FOOT
Petasites spp.

- damp forested roadsides, flowering early spring

By summer we are more apt to see the big Dandelion-like seed heads than the flowers, and the handsome, big, hand-like leaves attract some attention.

PENSTEMON
Penstemon spp.

- most abundant in the mountains and dry Interior on rock bluffs and slides, flowering in late spring and early summer.

Because they tend to mass in colonies, and because each plant is usually free-flowering, Penstemons often make striking displays of mauve and lavender. Some bright blue-purple kinds are more solitary. Scouler's Penstemon is the common species of Interior road-sides.

MARIPOSA LILY

Calochortus macrocarpus (A)
Calochortus apiculatus (B)

- dry Interior slopes in midsummer
Don't pick or dig this beautiful and distinctive plant, for you'll surely kill it! There are several other *Calochortus* kinds in the Pacific Northwest, mostly white or yellow.

A

B

Credit: Mrs. J.M. Woollett

PURPLE OYSTER PLANT

Tragopogon porrifolius

- common along dry, sunny roadsides, flowering late spring and early summer
Purple flowers give way to seed heads that resemble giant Dandelions. Slender blue-green foliage. Introduced from southern Europe. (See also page 25.)

Credit: Al and Jude Grass

Credit: B.C. Parks

SELF HEAL
Prunella vulgaris

- widespread on moist open ground to moderate elevations, blooming in early summer

The little spikes of hooded flowers are usually purplish, but do vary. They rise a few inches above a mat of rather pallid foliage.

WESTERN LONG-SPURRED VIOLET
Viola adunca

- open places, often amongst grass, flowering spring into summer

The flower color is variable, ranging from blue to nearly purple, and with pale and dark forms. The fine lines in the throat are similar to those in many other kinds of flowers. They are probably "honey guides" that lead insects to the nectar deep in the spur at the back of the flower. The plant gains by being pollenized. (See also page 17.)

Credit: Wm. Merilees

LUPINE
Lupinus spp.

- several kinds occur in showy blue colonies from the coast to high in the mountains in early summer

Most of our Lupine species are blue, with scattered pink or white variations, and we do have some yellowish kinds. All have similar, attractive palmate leaves.

Credit. Wm. Merilees

SHOWY JACOB'S LADDER
Polemonium pulcherrimum

- sporadic along roadsides, principally in the mountain passes, flowering in summer

The English name arises as a description of the plant's compound leaves, with their many opposite leaflets. Sniff the flowers and note their unpleasant smell.

BLUE-EYED MARY
Collinsia grandiflora

- conspicuous in spring on sunny rock bluffs by coastal roads and sometimes on ditchbanks further inland

Blue-eyed Mary is especially appealing when it blooms in mass with bright pink Sea Blush (see page 33).

CHICORY
Chicorium intybus

- widespread on dry ground at lower levels, flowers in summer

Chicory is an ancient food plant, brought here from Europe. The flowers open only in the morning, so the plant is easily missed.

MONKSHOOD
Aconitum columbianum

- damp places east of the coastal slopes, blooming in summer

This is usually found growing about one to two meters (four to six feet) tall, and has mild to deep blue flowers. It is poisonous, and sometimes a hazard to livestock, but a pleasure to the eye.

CAMAS

Camassia leichtlinii
Camassia quamash

- meadows and woodland edges in spring

Indians prized the edible bulbs of this bright blue lily, and sometimes fought for possession of the great patches that occur here and there in the Pacific Northwest.

Credit: B.C. Parks

WILD LARKSPUR

Delphinium spp.

- well-drained places from the coast into the mountains from late spring into summer

We have several kinds of these vivid blue-flowered plants. They contain strong toxins, and are of concern to stockmen when they occur on rangeland.

Credit: B.C. Parks

POISON IVY
Rhus radicans

- locally abundant in some Interior valleys, conspicuous only when red in autumn

Drooping leaves in threes, often with a few coarse teeth on the edges, identify Poison Ivy. Many people are sensitive to an oil it contains. Don't confuse it with harmless Sarsparilla, which has longer leaves with many fine teeth.

Credit: Wm. Merilees

SLENDER BOG ORCHID
Habenaria saccata

- damp open places and ditches in summer

Indians of some groups rubbed themselves or their guns with this strong-smelling plant, to gain luck in love or hunting.

CHOCOLATE LILY
Fritillaria lanceolata

- grassy woodland edge in spring and early summer

This is also called "Rice Root" because of the little white bulblets that surround the main mature bulb.

SUMAC
Rhus glabra

- conspicuous in dry Interior valleys, especially in autumn

In most years Sumac can outdo the Vine Maple of western slopes for intensity of color. Lewis Clark tells us that Sumac's name comes from the Arabic, and is not an Indian word as many have supposed.

Index to Scientific and Common Names